◯ human rights *first*

I0115857

Arbitrary Justice

Trials of Guantánamo and Bagram Detainees in Afghanistan

April 2008

Table of Contents

About Us

Human Rights First believes that building respect for human rights and the rule of law will help ensure the dignity to which every individual is entitled and will stem tyranny, extremism, intolerance, and violence.

Human Rights First protects people at risk: refugees who flee persecution, victims of crimes against humanity or other mass human rights violations, victims of discrimination, those whose rights are eroded in the name of national security, and human rights advocates who are targeted for defending the rights of others. These groups are often the first victims of societal instability and breakdown; their treatment is a harbinger of wider-scale repression. Human Rights First works to prevent violations against these groups and to seek justice and accountability for violations against them.

Human Rights First is practical and effective. We advocate for change at the highest levels of national and international policymaking. We seek justice through the courts. We raise awareness and understanding through the media. We build coalitions among those with divergent views. And we mobilize people to act.

Human Rights First is a non-profit, nonpartisan international human rights organization based in New York and Washington D.C. To maintain our independence, we accept no government funding.

Acknowledgements

This report was researched and written by Sahr MuhammedAlly, Senior Associate in the Law and Security Program at Human Rights First. The report was edited by Kevin Lanigan. Comments were also provided by Maureen Byrnes, Gabor Rona, Deborah Colson, and Devon Chaffee. Melissa Koven provided research assistance. Carly Beth Goodman and Sofia Rahman provided proofreading assistance and Sarah Graham provided production assistance. Additional comments were provided by Jonathon Horowitz of One World Research. Dr. Farouk Samim provided translation assistance.

Human Rights First would like to thank all those who spoke with us. We are particularly grateful to family members of former Guantánamo detainees and a former Block D defendant who shared their stories with us. We are grateful to the International Legal Foundation-Afghanistan, Afghan Human Rights Organization, and the numerous Afghan and U.S. government officials who spoke with us.

We would also like to thank the law firm Dechert LLP, the Center for Constitutional Rights, the International Justice Network, and One World Research.

Human Rights First gratefully acknowledges the generous support of The Atlantic Philanthropies, JEHT Foundation, John Merck Fund, Open Society Institute, and The Overbrook Foundation.

This report is available for free online at
www.humanrightsfirst.org

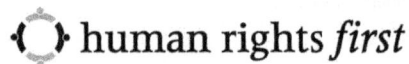

{ } human rights *first*

Headquarters

333 Seventh Avenue
13th Floor
New York, NY 10001-5108

Tel.: 212.845.5200
Fax: 212.845.5299

www.humanrightsfirst.org

Washington D.C. Office

100 Maryland Avenue, NE
Suite 500
Washington, DC 20002-5625

Tel: 202.547.5692
Fax: 202.543.5999

I. Executive Summary

About this Report

Human Rights First conducted research for this report in January-February 2008 in Kabul, Afghanistan, and follow-up research from New York. Human Rights First interviewed family members of Guantánamo returnees, a Block D defendant, defense lawyers, Afghan government officials, including prosecutors and judges, and officials from the U.S. embassy in Kabul. Human Rights First also observed two trials and examined court documents.

"I had goggles put over my eyes, I was handcuffed, and my legs were chained to the floor of the plane. The plane left Guantánamo and I arrived in Bagram. When we arrived, they took the goggles off and took my picture. I recognized that I was in Bagram, in Afghanistan. I had been here before . . . . The goggles were over my eyes again and we were taken to Pul-i-Charkhi . . . . I don't know who greeted us but I heard Dari. We were taken inside. They took the goggles off . . . . I [then] saw ANA [Afghan National Army] soldiers."

Human Rights First interview with Guantánamo returnee, Kabul, January 30, 2008
(describing his August 2007 return from Guantánamo to Afghanistan).

Blindfolded and handcuffed, detainees from Guantánamo Bay, Cuba, and Bagram Airfield, Afghanistan, are handed over by the United States to the Afghan government. After years of imprisonment without due process, the United States has concluded that their continued detention by U.S. authorities is no longer necessary. As the calls to close Guantánamo continue—including by U.S. Secretary of Defense Robert Gates, U.S. Secretary of State Condoleezza Rice, and Republican and Democratic presidential candidates—the transfer of detainees to their country of origin is not entirely without peril.[1] Since 2007, Afghans transferred by the United States to the Afghan government have been and are continuing to be prosecuted based on allegations by the United States, with little evidence. Prosecutions have resulted in convictions for most in proceedings that fail to meet international or even Afghan fair trial standards.

At this writing, over 30 Afghans remain in Guantánamo, down from approximately 200 in 2002. Similar transfers to other countries have reduced Guantánamo's overall prison population from over 750 at its peak to 280 today. But another 600 remain at the U.S. military's Bagram Theater Internment Facility (BTIF) in Afghanistan.

Facilitating the transfer of detainees to their home country is one way to close Guantánamo and other U.S. detention facilities, but transfers must be done responsibly.

This report looks at the arrangement between the United States and Afghan governments under which some Afghans in U.S. custody—both from Guantánamo and Bagram—are being transferred to the Afghan government for criminal prosecution. Based on first-hand interviews, examination of court documents, and trial observations in Kabul, Afghanistan, the report describes how Afghans

Bagram—The Other Guantánamo

While the U.S. detention camps at Guantánamo are well known, the same cannot be said for the U.S. military detention facility in Afghanistan—the Bagram Theater Internment Facility in Bagram Air Field (BAF). BAF is the largest Coalition and U.S. military base in Afghanistan. The Bagram Theater Internment Facility, under U.S. military control, now holds, without charge or trial, more than twice the number of detainees in Guantánamo.

transferred from U.S. custody are being charged and tried under Afghan law based on allegations, but little else, provided by the United States.

In April 2007, the Afghan National Detention Facility (ANDF) began operating in Pul-i-Charkhi prison located in the outskirts of Kabul. Known locally as "Block D," the detention facility was built by the U.S. government for Afghans to hold and prosecute former Guantánamo and Bagram detainees under Afghan law. The Afghan decision to prosecute, however, actually represented a rebuff to pressure by U.S. officials for the Afghans to detain transferred "enemy combatants" indefinitely, along the lines the United States has employed in Guantánamo and other detention facilities. Instead, an agreement was reached between Afghan and U.S. officials under which Afghanistan would prosecute the transferred detainees in Afghan courts.

At this writing, according to Afghan government officials, more than 250 former Guantánamo and Bagram detainees have been transferred to Block D. More than 160 have been referred for prosecution, while charges against the rest have not yet been finalized. The detainees are being charged under Afghan law for crimes ranging from treason and destruction of government property to threatening the security of Afghanistan. Trials last between 30 minutes to an hour and defendants have been sentenced to terms of imprisonment ranging from 3 to 20 years.

Human Rights First observed two trials and examined the evidence that was the basis of the court's judgments. The two cases lacked credible evidence to support the charges. The evidence presented included:

- A summary description of the circumstances of initial arrest read out in court by the prosecution and judge;

- A photograph provided by U.S. officials of an explosive or gun allegedly found at the time of arrest, without any information regarding witnesses or chain of custody;

- A statement by the defendant taken by the Afghan National Directorate of Security (NDS)—the Afghan national intelligence agency—and a national security prosecutor; and

- A statement by NDS summarizing vague findings arrived at several years after the date of arrest.

Based on information provided by Afghan judges, prosecutors, and defense lawyers, the experience of these two trials observed by Human Rights First was not unique. We were told that these trials were representative of Block D trials. Since the trials began in October 2007, 65 persons have been convicted in violation of fair trial standards based on allegations and evidence provided by the United States and supplemented by the Afghans; 17 have been acquitted.

During the trials, there are no prosecution witnesses presented, no out-of-court sworn prosecution witness statements to support the charges, and little or no physical evidence is presented. Defense counsel is not present when his client is interrogated by the prosecution, nor when the local NDS office attempts to collect evidence about a suspect as required by Afghan law. Defendants are thus unable to effectively challenge the evidence against them or cross-examine witnesses to the allegation, either in the pre-trial investigatory phase or during trial as allowed by Afghan law. Lawyers, in fact, are appointed to the case only after the investigation is concluded and generally have five days to review the government's evidence prior to trial, thereby impeding counsel from adequately preparing for trial. Such trials violate both Afghan criminal procedure law and international fair trial standards. And the outcomes of these trials—the acquittals as well as the convictions—appear entirely arbitrary.

Human Rights First has long advocated the importance of adherence to international fair trial standards, and the transfer of detainees to their country of origin, provided that there is no risk of torture or ill-treatment upon return. Where there is evidence of criminal activity, persons should be tried in proceedings that comport with international fair trial standards. In Afghanistan, the trials of former Bagram and Guantánamo detainees being conducted since October 2007 fall far short of this mark.

It should be noted that at this writing, Human Rights First is aware of no evidence that Guantánamo or Bagram returnees in Block D are being mistreated by the Afghan government. In addition, we applaud the Afghan government's decision to use its regular criminal justice system as the mechanism for adjudicating the guilt or innocence of these detainees. And finally, Human Rights First supports the transfer of detainees, as here, from isolated and indefinite U.S. custody to the custody of their home country governments, where they can renew contacts with family, and be subjected to an actual legal process rather than indefinite imprisonment. But it is critical that trials meet international fair trial standards.

The United States is one of the largest donors underwriting justice sector reforms in Afghanistan, and has for years been involved in drafting laws; training and equipping the national police force; renovating and building justice sector facilities throughout the country; and training judges, prosecutors and defense counsel on criminal justice, human rights, and rule of law issues. At a panel discussion on Afghan judicial reform in March 2008, Ambassador Thomas Schweich, Coordinator on Counternarcotics and Justice Reform in Afghanistan, in response to a question regarding criminal trials in Afghanistan, said that sometimes people are accused of a crime but "mere accusation does not mean guilt . . .

one needs evidence in court."[2] This principle should apply with equal force to the trials of Bagram and Guantánamo defendants. The United States should not undermine its own judicial reform efforts in Afghanistan by being complicit in fair trial violations.

The U.S. government, which detained, interrogated, and imprisoned these persons, in many cases, for years—and now appears to encourage Afghan government criminal prosecutions and continued detention—should take steps to support legitimate prosecutions in the Afghan courts.

Human Rights First makes the following recommendations to the governments of Afghanistan and the United States:

To the United States Department of Defense

- Provide non-classified information, including exculpatory evidence, to the Afghan authorities to assist in criminal prosecutions. Specifically:

  - Make available to Afghan officials the names of soldiers or other personnel involved in the apprehension of each detainee, witnesses to the alleged offense, and personnel involved in any interrogation of the detainee resulting in admissions or statements relevant to alleged offenses by the detainees, and make soldiers and or witnesses reasonably available for testimony, through video teleconference if necessary, for criminal proceedings; and

  - Provide Afghan authorities all statements by the transferred detainee; all reports, summaries, notes or other records of interrogation of the detainee; and any physical or documentary evidence in the possession of the U.S. government regarding each transferred detainee, including, for example, notes, seized weapons or ammunition.

- Refrain from transferring any evidence obtained through coercion or cruel, inhuman or degrading treatment for use in criminal prosecutions by other governments.

- For detainees apprehended in the future: ensure that units participating in operations likely to result in the detention of civilians include personnel trained and equipped for elementary evidence collection procedures, in order to better ensure that detainees transferred to the Afghan government for prosecution can be lawfully prosecuted.

- Establish a legal support operation in Kabul to support the legitimate prosecution in Afghan courts of detainees transferred by the United States.

To the Afghan Attorney General's office and the National Directorate of Security

- Request all relevant evidence in the possession of U.S. authorities, including exculpatory, regarding a detainee be turned over to Afghan officials at the time of transfer.

To the Afghan Supreme Court and Ministry of Justice

- Direct judges presiding over prosecutions of detainees transferred by the U.S. military to apply, and comply with, the Afghan criminal procedure code and international fair trial standards. Specifically, the Afghan courts in these cases should:

  - Ensure that defense counsel has access to all information that will be relied upon by the prosecution during trial;

  - Allow defense counsel to be present during the questioning of a defendant by the investigator and prosecutor prior to trial;

  - Require in-court witness testimony and allow cross-examination of witnesses by defense counsel; and

- Refrain from relying upon any defendant's statement to U.S. or Afghan officials unless the defendant confesses in court under oath and without compulsion—as required by both the Afghan Constitution and criminal procedure code.

To the Afghan Supreme Court and Ministry of Defense

- Ensure that trials of former Guantánamo and Bagram defendants are open to observers, including family members, and the media.

II. Guantánamo and Bagram Detentions

Following the U.S. invasion of Afghanistan in October 2001, the United States captured and transferred over 750 persons to Guantánamo Bay, Cuba. In 2007, 35 Afghans from Guantánamo were returned to Afghanistan.[3] At its peak, there were 200 Afghans in Guantánamo—more than 30 remain as of April 2008. In contrast, more than 600 persons are being held in U.S. military custody in Bagram Air Field.

The United States has slowly been transferring many Guantánamo detainees back to their home countries. At this writing, 280 men are still imprisoned in Guantánamo—almost all detained now for five or six years—all without trial. The Bush Administration has indicated that it ultimately intends to prosecute 80 persons detained in Guantánamo before its military commissions, although at this writing only 15 have been charged, and to date no trials have begun.[4]

Following the U.S. invasion in Afghanistan, many detainees initially were held in Bagram and then transferred to Guantánamo. Soon after the U.S. Supreme Court decisions in *Rasul v. Bush*, 542 U.S. 466 (2004) and *Hamdi v. Rumsfeld*, 542 U.S. 507 (2004), which recognized limited rights of Guantánamo detainees to challenge their detentions in U.S. courts, transfers from Bagram to Guantánamo declined.

"Unlawful Enemy Combatant"

The United States government defines "unlawful enemy combatant" as "a person who has engaged in hostilities or who has purposefully and materially supported hostilities against the United States or its co-belligerents who is not a lawful enemy combatant (including a person who is part of the Taliban, al Qaeda, or associated forces)."[5]

The Bush Administration asserts that "unlawful enemy combatants" can be held pursuant to the President's powers as commander-in-chief and under the laws of war until the end of hostilities. The administration argues that detaining enemy combatants prevents them from returning to the battlefield, thereby deterring further armed attacks, and allows the United States to gather intelligence through interrogation to prevent future attacks.[6]

Detainees sent by the United States to Guantánamo were not afforded any individualized determination of Prisoner of War status before a competent tribunal, as provided by Article 5 of the Third Geneva Convention. The Bush Administration has consistently stated that persons held in Bagram and Guantánamo, including Taliban members, are categorically not prisoners of war and thus not entitled to Article 5 hearings. Following the *Rasul* and *Hamdi* Supreme Court decisions, the Department of Defense began conducting Combatant Status Review Tribunal (CSRT) hearings for Guantánamo detainees.[7] Detainees in CSRTs are not provided lawyers, are given only a summary of the allegations against them, and have in all cases been denied requests to bring in outside witnesses to help establish their innocence. CSRTs may also review secret evidence that detainees are unable to confront. The U.S. government also set up Administrative Review Boards (ARBs) to annually review each detainee's CSRT-designated status as an enemy combatant.[8]

According to U.S. government court filings in U.S. District Court, for persons transferred to Bagram a panel of five U.S. military officers, sitting as the Enemy Combatant Review Board (ECRB), review the detainees' status usually within 75 days of their capture and thereafter every six months.[9] The ECRB may recommend by a majority vote to the Commanding General or his designee on the detainee's status after reviewing evidence. Much of the evidence before the ECRBs is culled from military personnel involved in the capture.[10] The evidence relied upon by the ECRB includes "testimony from individuals involved in the capture and interrogation of the detainee."[11] The detainee generally does not appear before the ECRB at either the initial status hearing or the bi-annual review.[12]

U.S.-Afghan Relationship Regarding Detainees

The U.S. military exercises control over detainees in U.S. custody in Afghanistan, ostensibly pursuant to the May 23, 2005, Joint Declaration of the United States-Afghanistan Strategic Partnership (Joint Declaration).[13] However, there actually is no express authorization in the Joint Declaration for U.S. detainee operations in Afghanistan. The closest the document comes to addressing the topic is its statement that "U.S. military forces operating in Afghanistan will continue to have access to Bagram Air Base and its facilities, and facilities at other locations as may be mutually determined and . . . the U.S. and Coalition Forces are to continue to have the freedom of action required to conduct appropriate military operations."[14]

The Joint Declaration, however, does address detainee operations by the Afghan government: "As Afghan Government capabilities increase . . . the Afghan Government intends to maintain capabilities for the detention, as appropriate, of persons apprehended in the War on Terror."[15] Thus, in August 2005, the Afghan and U.S. governments entered into a bilateral agreement through an exchange of diplomatic notes (the 2005 Notes) that set forth conditions for the transfer of Afghan detainees in United States custody to the Afghan government. The 2005 Notes are not available publicly, but a reference to an agreement between the two countries regarding detainees— that is, this exchange of notes—is contained in a U.S. Embassy Kabul press release, dated August 4, 2005, which states:

> During their May 2005 meetings, President Bush and President Karzai expressed a strong desire to return Afghan detainees to Afghanistan as part of the U.S.-Afghanistan Strategic Partnership.
>
> Today, in beginning to implement the Joint Declaration on Strategic Partnership, Afghanistan and the United States reached an understanding that will allow for the gradual transfer of Afghan detainees to the exclusive custody and control of the Afghan Government.
>
> The Government of Afghanistan will accept responsibility for the returning Afghan citizens and will work to ensure that they do not pose a continuing threat to Afghanistan, the Coalition, or the international community as a whole. The United States is prepared to assist Afghanistan in capacity building, including infrastructure, and to provide training, as appropriate.[16]

According to the *New York Times*, which has a draft of the 2005 Notes, Washington has asked Kabul to share intelligence information from the detainees, "utilize all methods appropriate and permissible under Afghan law to surveil or monitor their activities following any release," and "confiscate or deny passports and take measures to prevent each national from traveling outside Afghanistan."[17] As part of the accord, the United States said it would finance the rebuilding of an Afghan prison block and help equip and train an Afghan guard force.[18] Block D in Pul-i-Charkhi is that prison block.

U.S. Involvement in Justice Sector Reform in Afghanistan

The construction of Block D is far from the only major expenditure by the United States on "justice sector" development in Afghanistan. On December 5, 2001, the international community concluded a United Nations Security Council endorsed Agreement on Provisional Arrangement in Afghanistan Pending the Re-establishment of Permanent Government Institutions (Bonn Agreement). The parties to the Bonn Agreement stipulated that achieving the rule of law was a fundamental and central goal among reconstruction efforts in Afghanistan.[19] In general, Italy was charged with reforming the Afghan judicial system. Germany was charged with developing the Afghan National Police. The United States was given the mandate to reform the Afghan National Army (ANA), including military law reform.[20]

The United States is one of the largest donors to justice sector reform in Afghanistan. After thirty years of conflict, the formal Afghan justice sector is weak and faces serious difficulties, including poor infrastructure, inadequate training and education, lack of access to laws and textbooks, lack of public defenders, and institutionalized corruption. According to the 2007 United Nations Human Development Report, only about half of the judges have the relevant formal higher education.[21]

The United States is involved in rule of law issues primarily through four agencies: the Department of Defense (DOD), the Department of State/Bureau for International Narcotics and Law Enforcement Affairs (INL), the U.S. Agency for International Development (USAID), and the Department of Justice.

DOD coordinates military justice reform through the Combined Security Transition Command-Afghanistan (CTSC-A). U.S. advisors are involved in legal drafting, training, and mentoring the ANA, ANP, and the Ministry of Defense.[22]

The State Department provides technical and advisory support for Afghan justice administrators such as the Ministry of Justice, Ministry of Interior, the Attorney General's office, and the Supreme Court. The INL's Justice Sector Support Program provides legal counsel and mentoring to prosecutors, judges, and defense counsel focusing on Afghan and international law, human rights, and criminal justice procedures.[23] The mentoring also includes training to improve investigations, police-prosecutor coordination, case management, trial advocacy, and adjudication of criminal cases.[24] U.S. advisors are presently involved in supporting the revision of the Afghan 2004 Interim Criminal Procedure Code for Courts (ICPC).[25]

Justice Department Senior Federal Prosecutor Program in Kabul provides law reform advice, training, mentoring, and support of the Afghan counternarcotics task force of prosecutors and police. USAID is involved in supporting reform of the civil and commercial law sectors.

Notwithstanding the Afghan commitment in the Joint Declaration, it was—and remains—unclear under what legal authority the Afghan government may detain persons transferred by the United States and housed in Block D. Afghan officials rejected suggestions by U.S. officials that the Afghan government simply assert authority to detain "enemy combatants" indefinitely as the U.S. government has done in Guantánamo.[26]

Instead, an agreement was reached between the two governments that the Afghan government would prosecute Guantánamo and Bagram detainees in Afghan courts under Afghan law. An Afghan official explained to Human Rights First that, according to the agreement

between Afghan and U.S. authorities, detainees from Guantánamo and Bagram are to be transferred to Block D for prosecutions.[27] A team of National Directorate Security investigators and prosecutors visit Bagram and along with U.S. authorities "filter cases for prosecution."[28] The two governments decide which detainees should be prosecuted and which can be released directly from Bagram through the Afghan National Commission for Peace and Reconciliation—the official entity charged with reintegrating into society members of the armed opposition to the Afghan government.[29]

III. Block D, Pul-i-Charkhi

Afghan National Army guards outside Block D, Pul-i-Charkhi prison, Afghanistan (Photo MASSOUD HOSSAINI/AFP/Getty Images)

The United States has spent over $20 million in constructing Block D and has earmarked an additional $18 million for three years to train and mentor Afghan National Army guards to run the detention center.[30] Although the Afghan Ministry of Justice (MOJ) generally has oversight function of prisons and detention centers, including Pul-i-Charkhi which has other prisons, Block D is operated by the Ministry of Defense (MOD) and not the Ministry of Justice.

An Afghan National Detention Facility task force is composed of representatives from the Afghan National Security Council,[31] NDS, Attorney General, MOD, MOJ, and the U.S. embassy to assess who is transferred for criminal prosecution. In interviews with Human Rights First, both U.S. and Afghan officials characterized the U.S. role in the ANDF task force as one of "mentoring" the Afghans.

On March 2, 2008, President Hamid Karzai issued a Presidential Decree (attached as Appendix B) creating an intra-agency committee to review complaints of former Bagram and Guantánamo detainees now in Block D. According to the decree, Members of the Supreme Court, MOD, NDS, and MOJ will "check the complaints, problems, documents and files" of the defendants and submit their report to the president.[32] The committee is mandated to review a detainee's file consisting of information provided by the U.S. and Afghan officials, and recommend release post-conviction, or affirm the court's verdict, or recommend continued detention. To date, the committee has reviewed 120 cases and recommended release of 53 people, but no one has been released yet. [33] A committee member told Human Rights First that, "we have to be fair, the committee will recommend that these people have legal representation."[34]

Conditions of Confinement

There are 350 cells in Block D and, at this writing, each cell is occupied by only one person.[35] Block D can hold up to 700 detainees if there are two persons in each cell.

The International Committee of the Red Cross (ICRC) and the United Nations Assistance Mission in Afghanistan (UNAMA) both have access to detainees in Block D. (ICRC also has access to the Bagram Theater Internment Facility, but UNAMA officials do not). Compared to other Afghan prisons and NDS detention facilities, where detainees allegedly have been subjected to torture and ill-treatment, to date there have been no such complaints about Block D.[36]

According to Afghan officials and a former Block D detainee, detainees are flown from Guantánamo to the U.S. military's Bagram Air Field and then transported by U.S. military helicopter to Afghan officials in Block D. Upon arrival in Block D, detainees are kept on the third floor for observation and not allowed to interact with other detainees, or meet visitors, or have time outside the cell.[37] If a detainee is cooperative and observes prison rules, then he is moved to the second floor and is allowed to pray in *jamat* (collectively) with other detainees, allowed visitors twice a week, and permitted exercise three days a week.[38] A detainee on the first floor has the most privileges and is allowed to watch television, can be outside his cell from 8:00 a.m. to 10:00 p.m., can pray collectively, and receive visitors daily.[39] A detainee is moved between the floors, gaining and losing privileges, depending on his behavior and cooperation.

As of February 4, 2008, two former Bagram detainees were still on the third floor—one, as explained by an ANA official to Human Rights First because he was non-cooperative, and the other because of "mental issues."[40]

Family Visits

Human Rights First met with family members of Guantánamo transferees. Each family member expressed a sense of relief that their relative was back in Afghanistan and they were finally able to meet with them. Redacted ICRC letters were the only form of communication between the family and a detainee during as many as five or six years in U.S. custody.[41] (In January 2008, the ICRC, in coordination with the United States, setup a call center at its Kabul office for families to communicate with Bagram detainees).[42]

Some family members told Human Rights First that they were under the impression that detainees were found "innocent" in Guantánamo, thus leading to their return to Afghanistan. They were therefore understandably confused as to why their family member had not returned home and remained detained in Afghanistan with the possibility of being prosecuted.[43]

Human Rights First spoke to the brother of a Guantánamo detainee, who, according to the brother, had traveled to Pakistan to buy supplies for the family auto spare-parts shop, but was arrested by Pakistani authorities and then transferred to U.S. custody. His brother has been detained for more than five years in Guantánamo and in 2007 was transferred to Block D. He lamented the lost time with his brother and said:

> The reason why he was transferred to Afghanistan is because they [the U.S.] did not find any evidence against him. My brother does not know the charges against him. Perhaps the Pakistanis have accused him. I don't know why my brother is still in jail. If my brother has committed a crime he should be punished, but he spent five and a half years in jail for what? . . . Tell us what he has done. What are the charges? Let us know the sentence so we know how much longer to wait. If convicted—fine we need to know. My brother is married, he has two sons who are eight and nine and a daughter who is six years old. The children visited their father [in Block D], but they did not feel close to him because they have not seen him in over five years. My brother was very sad. But I told him it will take time.[44]

Visiting rooms for Block D detainees, as described by family members of detainees, appear to be similar to a visiting room in a U.S. prison. The visiting rooms are divided in half by a glass wall. The glass wall has holes through which the detainee and visitor can converse.[45] Unarmed ANA guards are on each side of the glass wall. Detainees are not handcuffed during visits but wear ankle chains. Visits last 20 to 30 minutes. Family members described seeing cameras in the visiting room.[46]

A brother of a Guantánamo detainee described seeing his brother for the first time in six years:

> Two weeks after he was brought to Block D, I saw him . . . . The room was divided by glass panel. It had small holes. I shook hands with my brother with two fingers through the holes. When I entered the room and saw him it was unbelievable. It was sad to see my brother. He was limping. He had chains on his ankles. He is younger than me but looked older. I could not believe it was him.[47]

My brother was in Guantánamo for five years. . . . When he was taken by the Americans we thought he had disappeared, that he was dead. We did not know where he was . . . .No one would tell us . . . . Three months later we got a letter from my brother through the ICRC.

We don't blame the Americans for arrest. They don't have personal anomosity against my family, but they were given the wrong information. This is a problem. But no one can coordinate with the Americans; to go to the village to find out about my brother. What sort of a man he is so my brother can come home.

– Human Rights First interview with brother (name withheld) of a Guantánamo returnee, Kabul, January 31, 2008.

IV. Prosecution of Guantánamo and Bagram Detainees

According to Afghan government sources, as of April 1, 2008, 250 detainees have been transferred to Block D, of which 160 have been referred for prosecution. There have been 65 convictions—40 have been sentenced from 3 to 20 years imprisonment and 25 have been sentenced to time-served. There have been 17 acquittals. In these trials there are no prosecution witnesses to support the allegations. The verdicts of these trials appear entirely arbitrary.

Detainees in Block D are tried under the 1987 Law of Crimes Against the Internal and External Security of the Democratic Republic of Afghanistan (Internal and External Security Code). This law was enacted during the rule of the Soviet Union-supported Communist government of Afghanistan. Detainees have been charged with crimes including:

- treason (article 1)—punishable by death or life sentence;

- destruction of government and private property by explosives (article 5)—punishable by 10 to 20 years;

- organizing activity against the internal and external security (article 9)—punishable by life sentence; and

- assisting the enemy forces (article 23)—which carries a sentence not exceeding ten years.

The Role of the National Directorate of Security in Investigations

After transfer by the U.S. military of the Guantánamo or Bagram detainee, along with the evidence, further investigations of Block D detainees are carried out by Afghanistan's national intelligence agency, the National Directorate of Security. The NDS is one of the largest security sector agencies in Afghanistan. Its headquarters are in Kabul and it has sub-offices throughout the country. It receives aid and training from the German and U.S. governments.[48] The investigating arm of the NDS—Department 17—is responsible for investigating the offenses, based on allegations by the United States, of the Guantánamo and Bagram detainees. A national security prosecutor then decides what charges to file against a detainee.

There reportedly is a classified presidential decree that sets out the NDS' mandate. In practice, the NDS appears to have a broad mandate that includes detention, interrogation, and investigation of persons alleged to have committed crimes against national security. In November 2007, during a visit to Afghanistan, Louise Arbour, the United Nations High Commissioner for Human Rights, noted her concern about NDS, "given that it is not a regular law enforcement body and operates on the basis of a secret decree. . . . [and] urged the President to ensure greater transparency, access to, and accountability of this institution, starting with publication of the decree on which its powers are based." [49]

The Evidence

Afghan government prosecutors told Human Rights First that the U.S. government provides the Afghans with the basic "evidence" which forms the foundation for the Afghan charges against the transferred Guantánamo and Bagram detainees. U.S. authorities provide their Afghan counterparts with a file on each detainee. The file contains an Unclassified English version of the "Detainee Assessment Branch Report of Investigation" (ROI) (a copy of a ROI is available at Appendix C). The file also contains an unofficial translation of the ROI in Dari, and photographs of evidence, if any, allegedly seized with the detainee at the time of capture.

Human Rights First has examined the trial dossiers of two defendants. The ROIs are highly general and state the date of capture, by whom (e.g., Coalition Forces, Afghan National Army or Afghan National Police), and what the detainee was alleged to have done. Prosecutors and lawyers confirmed that sometimes the name of an American appears in the files, for example, the name of the U.S. military judge advocate (lawyer) who reviewed the investigation form. [50] But there are no names of individual witnesses other than perhaps another detainee captured at the same time. Sometimes witnesses are identified simply as "Coalition Forces" or "ANA" or "ANP." There also are no statements in the court dossier—sworn or unsworn—of any U.S. soldiers or officials involved in the capture or interrogation of the detainee.

Civil Law System in Afghanistan

Afghanistan's criminal procedure is based on civil law. Fact-finding is done by the investigative prosecutor (primary *saranwal*) who plays the role of an inquisitor whose objective is to ascertain the truth, and has broad powers to compel testimony, seek out experts, and collect and preserve evidence. [51] The prosecutor must seek out both exculpatory and inculpatory evidence in order to assess whether there is sufficient evidence for trial. [52] All evidence collected and testimony taken are compiled in a written dossier and submitted to the judges appointed to the case. During the investigative phase, the accused and the accused's lawyer have the right to be present while the investigative prosecutor collects evidence. [53] If the case is referred to trial, everything contained in the dossier constitutes evidence, and the trial court is entitled to treat all witness testimony in the investigative dossier as having been given at trial.

A former Bagram detainee's dossier also may contain a summary of the review before the Enemy Combatant Review Board. For instance, in one case we examined, an ECRB concluded that a detainee was a "Low Threat LLEC [Low Level Enemy Combatant]" and the ECRB's assessment is "Low Threat to US/CF [Coalition Forces]/Low Prosecution Value." (See Appendix D). Upon transfer to the Afghans for prosecution, this detainee was charged with destruction (article 5 of the Internal and External Security Code), convicted, and sentenced to eight years. There were no witnesses at trial.

Both Afghan prosecutors and defense lawyers told Human Rights First that there is very little real evidence provided by U.S. authorities. One lawyer stated:

> Evidence is slim. It's given to the Afghans by the Americans. For instance, the file will mention a car, but no license plate, or some say guns, but where is the gun or ammunition. We review a file with typed notes in English with translation in Dari, but the evidence itself is not that much. [54]

Another defense lawyer said:

> The evidence used against the defendants is usually very weak and there is usually not a lot of it. For example, one client was charged with having a weapon and in his file there was a picture of the weapon. But the actual weapon was not provided. There were no details about the type of weapon or who arrested him. What he was doing with the weapon.[55]

One defense counsel stated that when he questions the validity of the evidence during trial, the prosecutors' standard response is:

> Why would the Americans detain him then? The U.S. has nothing against this person unless he's guilty."[56]

After receiving the evidence files from U.S. authorities, the Afghan authorities then conduct their own cursory investigation. "As raw materials we use the evidence from the U.S.," explained a national security prosecutor.[57] Department 17 of the NDS (the investigatory branch of NDS) in Kabul then sends a letter of inquiry to the local NDS office nearest to the detainee's hometown and/or place of capture, asking if there is any information about the detainee's alleged crime. The local NDS official sends a letter to Department 17 summarizing their findings. Human Rights First examined information in several cases provided by the local NDS offices. Based on our review of these files and discussion with counsel, it is clear that the NDS investigation is very superficial and based on second-, or even third-hand information. Again, there are no sworn witness statements.

The NDS investigative department and a national security investigative prosecutor then interview the defendant and write up the indictment based on information provided by the local NDS office and the United States.[58] One former Block D defendant—who was tried without counsel—told Human Rights First that he was interviewed by the prosecutor only once before his trial.[59]

One lawyer stated that "prosecutors actually have a difficult time in putting together charges because of the weak evidence."[60] Despite this observation, the weak evidence has resulted in far more convictions than acquittals. This can be explained by the trial judges' inclination in a civil law system to rely heavily on the prosecutor—which obviously works best when the prosecutor is fulfilling his responsibility to be objective and not adversarial in the case, and is diligent in constructing a case based on real evidence. In these trials, while in theory there is a presumption of innocence, in practice, the burden appears to be entirely on the accused to prove his innocence, and the means to do so are scant. In response to a question by Human Rights First regarding challenges by defense counsel to weight of the evidence, a judge explained:

> The information comes from the Coalition Forces. We are sure that these people arrested were not arrested for nothing. The U.S. is not lying.[61]

Human Rights First met with U.S. embassy officials in Kabul to discuss the proceedings, how evidence was being introduced in violation of the Afghan criminal procedure code and international law, and how defense lawyers' challenges to the evidence were not being considered by the court. An embassy official commented, "challenges based on evidence even on appeal will not be enough to overturn the verdict." "It would not be basis for reversal," he added.[62]

In addition to challenging the prosecution's case directly (discussed in section V), defense lawyers in these cases try to submit to the court their own letters from village and tribal elders and provincial council members attesting to the defendants' innocence. One defense lawyer told Human Rights First, "We try to collect evidence. For example, if a family is in Gardez, we contact them to get letters from elders in the village and local governors who can attest to the innocence and guarantee that the person will be peaceful and not opposed to the government."[63] A judge, however, dismissed the validity of these letters and told Human Rights First that such letters "are not given much consideration in determining the guilt or innocence."[64] Such information, of course—when it supports guilt—from the same sources is exactly what is gathered by the NDS in the course of the Afghan government investigation. And these letters, from village elders and local governors, are relied upon by the Afghan government's National Commission for Peace and Reconciliation when negotiating the direct release of detainees from U.S. custody.[65]

"Guarantee Letters"

Detainees' family members have tried to show innocence by obtaining letters from village and tribal elders, as well as from the local member of government or governor attesting to the innocence of the detainee. Some of these letters have been provided to *habeas* counsel in the United States, to be submitted to U.S. authorities on behalf of Guantánamo detainees. A brother of a Guantánamo detainee expressed the efforts taken to secure these letters, saying:

You know for each signature in the letters on my brother's behalf it took weeks and months. I was robbed because people said they will help me, but no one can help against the U.S.[66]

Another family member described his efforts to release his brother:

My brother is not Taliban or al Qaeda. Keeping innocent person for six years is persecution. No one cares about them. When I talk about my brother everyone says sorry. I have struggled so much. I have gone to the National Security Council, the Peace and Reconciliation Committee. They say yes it's sad, but no one can help us. I have all the guarantee letters signed by the district governor, elders and I took it to the Reconciliation Committee. They say they don't have the power. [67]

Observations of Trial Proceedings

Human Rights First attended two trials of Block D defendants. Both trials involved defendants who were detained by the U.S. military at Bagram. Each trial lasted about 30 minutes. In each trial, the prosecutor read the charges and his prepared statement, then defense counsel read a prepared statement, and a three-panel judge asked questions. The defendant responded to the judges' questions and made a statement as well—in both cases denying their guilt. No witness other than the defendant appeared or testified.

One judge read excerpts from a letter prepared by the NDS summarizing its findings. Neither the prosecutor nor any judge read any witness accounts or even mentioned the names of witnesses. Human Rights First examined the dossier of one these cases and saw no witness statements. Both defendants were convicted.

During each trial, Human Rights First observed that defense counsel raised several objections to the lack of evidence and witnesses to support the allegations and that the evidence was collected in violation of Afghan criminal procedure law. The judges did not respond to the defense counsel's legal objections.

Below are excerpts from an exchange between a judge and defense lawyer observed by Human Rights First:

Judge: Why then was your client arrested amongst so many others and why did people say he was a Talib, and why did the ANA [Afghan National Army] fire upon him in the garden?

Defense Lawyer: Where is the evidence that my client was in the area where the attack happened?

Prosecutor: Eyewitnesses said this right after the arrest and he was arrested in the act with a gun and radio.

Judge: How did the U.S. arrest him?

Prosecutor: It is America's job to do this if agreed upon by the Afghan government.

Defense Lawyer: Is there any eyewitness to this? Where is this person?

The trial lasted 30 minutes. The defendant was charged under article 23 (assisting enemy forces), convicted, and sentenced to ten years' imprisonment—the maximum sentence for the offense. The judge asked the defendant if he accepted the sentence. The defendant rejected the sentence and said that he wanted to appeal. The defendant was told that he had a right to appeal within 20 days and was instructed to put his thumbprint on the sentence slip. To date, no appeal has taken place.

V. Procedural Concerns in the Conduct of Trials

Based on interviews with key actors in the trial proceedings, our review of two dossiers, and observations of two trials, Human Rights First has identified procedural flaws that significantly undermine the fairness of the trials taking place in Block D, Pul-i-Charkhi.

Afghanistan became a party to the International Covenant of Civil and Political Rights (ICCPR) in 1983, and all successor governments remain bound by it. Article 14 of the ICCPR provides that any person charged with a criminal offense is entitled to a "fair and public hearing by a competent, independent and impartial tribunal established by law."[68] "A fair trial" under the ICCPR requires that a person being tried for a criminal offense must be guaranteed, at a minimum, the following rights:

- To be presumed innocent until proved guilty according to the law;

- To be informed of the charges against oneself in detail and promptly, in a language one understands;

- To have adequate time and facilities for the preparation of a defense and communication with counsel of one's own choosing;

- To be tried without undue delay; to be tried in one's own presence, and to defend oneself in person or through legal counsel of one's own choosing;

- To examine witnesses against oneself and be able to obtain the attendance and examination of witnesses on one's behalf, under the same conditions as the prosecution;

- Not to be compelled to confess guilt or incriminate oneself; and

- To be able to appeal to a higher tribunal against conviction and sentence.[69]

These fundamental fair trial principles are applicable irrespective of whether the legal system of the country conforms to a common law (such as in the United States and England) or civil law system (such as in Germany and Afghanistan). The procedural flaws identified by Human Rights First of Block D trials undermine several fair trial guarantees, including: the right to adequate time and facilities to prepare a defense; the right not to incriminate oneself; the right to be informed of charges in a language one can understand; and the right to examine witnesses against the accused.

Defendant's Right to Confront the Evidence

A defendant's right to examine the evidence and confront the witnesses is a fundamental fair trial guarantee. This is essential to test the credibility of the witnesses and their evidence. This right requires that an accused should be given "adequate and proper opportunity to challenge and question a witness against him, either at the time the witness makes the statement or at some later stage in the proceedings."[70] A conviction thus cannot be substantially based on the statements of witnesses whom the defense counsel is unable to cross-examine.

In a civil law system, witness testimony can be taken either during the investigation phase or at trial. During the investigation phase, the Afghan criminal procedure code provides for defense counsel and a defendant to be present during witness testimony, searches, confrontations, and line-up procedures, and this right can only be waived when there is urgent need to conduct the operations or concern for loss of evidence.[71] Afghan law mandates that "records of the testimonies of the witnesses . . . collected during the investigative phase, can have the value of evidence as basis for the decision only if . . . the accused and/or his defense counsel were present during the operations and were in a position to raise questions and make objections. Otherwise the related deeds have the sole value of clues."[72]

In practice, defense counsel is not present when his client is interrogated by the prosecution, nor when the local NDS office attempts to collect evidence about a suspect.

Lawyers are appointed to the case only after the investigation is concluded.

When asked whether defense counsel can interview U.S. soldiers involved in the arrest, a defense counsel replied, "With Americans it is very difficult. We don't know who the interrogator or soldier is. We do not meet the Americans. This is not allowed."[73] Even the Afghan prosecutors are in no better position than defense counsel when it comes to trying to get real evidence from U.S. authorities. As one national security prosecutor admitted, "we can't question U.S. soldiers or interrogators for Bagram or Guantánamo detainees" because so much time has elapsed since the date of capture.[74] The evidence "is all packaged and handed to us on a plate," the prosecutor added.[75]

Defense counsel are not only denied the opportunity to challenge evidence in the investigation phase, but because no prosecution witnesses testify in court, defendants are completely deprived of their rights to confront evidence. This situation is aggravated by the fact that the evidence in the dossier consists of second- and third-hand statements and summary allegations, with no names of witnesses who can be interviewed or brought to court and cross-examined.

Task Force 134

The U.S. military's Task Force 134 in Iraq is charged with assisting prosecutions in the Central Criminal Court of Iraq (CCCI). U.S. soldiers appear as witnesses in Iraqi courts, even through video teleconference, and U.S. judge advocates train soldiers and marines in collecting evidence for criminal prosecution in Iraqi courts.[76]

Human Rights First has not examined the trials at CCCI and cannot attest to the fairness of the proceedings. Nor have we examined the adequacy of the investigations to build a criminal case by Task Force 134. The comparison to Task Force 134 is to show that the U.S. military is engaged in evidence-gathering and makes soldiers available for testimony in Iraqi criminal trials of persons captured by the United States.

Moreover, defense counsel is not adequately able to prepare a defense when the evidence in the dossier consists of second- and third-hand statements and summary allegations with no names of witnesses who can be brought to court and cross-examined.

Use of Coerced Evidence

Guantánamo and Bagram detainees have reported being subjected to harsh treatment during confinement. As widely documented in human rights[77] and press reports,[78] including U.S. government documents,[79] detainees have been subjected to beatings; stress positions; sexual abuse and humiliation; sensory deprivation; sleep, food and water deprivation; exposure to cold temperature; isolation; dousing with cold water; and blaring of loud music.

A Block D defendant, who was sentenced to five years—initially a detainee in Bagram before being sent to Guantánamo and returned in 2007 to Block D—told Human Rights First about the conditions of confinement in Bagram in 2002:

I was in an isolation cell for two months. I could not talk to anyone. Loud English music was played all the time. It was bothersome. There were no windows. I had no water to do ablution for prayers. I did not know whether it was night or day. The light was on all the time.[80]

A Guantánamo returnee transferred to Block D, alleged in his Combatant Status Review Tribunal hearing in Guantánamo that, while in Bagram, he was physically abused, forced to stand for ten days, and not allowed to sit or sleep while his hands were tied.[81]

And as recently as 2007, the ICRC, as reported in the *New York Times*, complained that dozens of Bagram detainees were still being held incommunicado in isolation cells and not notified to the ICRC for as long as several months and some were subjected to cruel treatment during interrogations. [82]

This history is relevant to the Block D trials because it appears that detainee statements extracted by U.S. interrogators in coercive detention conditions—and thus inherently unreliable—may be infecting the Block D trials.[83] A defense lawyer expressed concern that a detainee's confession before U.S. or Afghan forces at the time of capture could be coerced. He stated:

> Prosecutors offer evidence to the trial of confessions which were obtained by the U.S., or ANA . . . at their initial capture, but were later retracted by the defendant. Sometimes these written or verbal confessions were obtained through different kinds of coercion, such as making the detainee stand in the rain or putting them in harsh prison conditions.[84]

Another defense lawyer expressed similar concerns regarding confessions, noting that the judges do not appear to take such challenges seriously:

> My clients have told me that they have been beaten at Bagram or at time of the arrest. When we mention this to the judge, the judge says that Bagram and Guantánamo detainees are exceptional cases because they are arrested by Coalition Forces and therefore they [Afghans] can't pay attention to issues of ill-treatment.[85]

But the Afghan Constitution prohibits introduction into evidence of statements obtained "by means of compulsion" and recognizes a confession as a voluntary admission only if taken before a judge.[86] The Afghan criminal procedure code similarly prohibits a suspect or accused from "undergo[ing] intimidations or any form of physical or psychological pressure."[87] And international law likewise prohibits the use of evidence procured by torture, or by cruel, inhuman or degrading treatment, in all legal proceedings.[88]

Access to Counsel and Preparation for Trial

When Block D trials commenced in October 2007, ten individuals were tried and convicted without defense counsel. According to a former Block D detainee who was tried, convicted, and sentenced without counsel, detainees complained to the ICRC about the lack of counsel.[89] A U.S. embassy official told Human Rights First that when the United States learned that some defendants were tried without counsel, they spoke with Afghan authorities to ensure legal aid is provided to the defendants.[90] Now six Afghan lawyers are representing more than 160 defendants.

Defense lawyers are allowed to meet with their clients privately, and there are no restrictions on the number of visits.[91] One lawyer noted that his clients at first were hesitant and did not know what role the lawyer would play. "Some detainees are cautious and not sure who we are and whether we can be trusted. I guess this is because they have been detained without a lawyer for many years in Bagram," said a defense lawyer.[92]

Defense counsel told Human Rights First that they usually are not allowed to review the court dossier until five days before trial. As noted above, except in exigent circumstances Afghan law requires defense counsel to be allowed to be present while the investigating prosecutor is taking witness testimony and gathering the evidence, so that he can become knowledgeable of the evidence to be presented in court. But Block D prosecutions are being conducted in disregard of these requirements. Defense counsel is appointed when a detainee has been charged and the dossier has been transferred to the court. A defense lawyer told Human Rights First, "I have not been present during the prosecutor's interrogation because my clients had representation [only] after the prosecutor [had already] asked [all] their questions."[93] Thus the timing of their appointment alone effectively impedes defense counsel in these proceedings from adequately preparing for trial.

Notably, in early February 2008 when Human Rights First met with lawyers representing Block D defendants we learned that they were unaware of CSRT and ARB proceedings in Guantánamo.

Lack of Interpreter During Trial

Dari and Pushto are the official languages of Afghanistan. Official business in Kabul, however, including court proceedings, is conducted more frequently in Dari. The Afghan criminal procedure code does obligate the court to provide an interpreter to a defendant during trial proceedings for "explaining to him the charge and the indictment and for assisting him during the interrogations and confrontations."[94] This is consistent with international fair trial standards.[95] According to defense lawyers, defendants in Block D are predominantly Pushto speakers, and there are no interpreters during trials. In one of the trials observed by Human Rights First, as the prosecutor began reading the opening statement, the defendant jumped up from his seat and made motions to defense counsel indicating that he could not understand. The defendant spoke only Pushto and did not speak or understand Dari.

The judges also read excerpts from the dossier—again, in Dari. Defense counsel told the court that his client did not speak Dari. Several times during the trial the defendant asked defense counsel to translate what was being said. The judges did speak Pushto and questioned the defendant in Pushto, but otherwise refused to conduct the proceeding in Pushto. The defendant, charged under article 5 (destruction), was convicted and sentenced to eight years. There were no witnesses and the trial lasted 35 minutes.

Release of Detainees Post Trial

Human Rights First was told by defense lawyers and a former Block D defendant that for defendants who were acquitted or sentenced to time-served, the delay before release can be from a few days to one month.

An official with the Supreme Court explained that following a verdict, the case is referred to the NDS and the attorney general's office. He, however, refused to elaborate on the details and said, "I don't know how much time the attorney general and NDS take to decide when to release someone and I don't want to talk about it."[96]

The new presidential committee established in March 2008 to look into Block D trials can also recommend release. But it appears that NDS does play a role in the release process.

Block D Defendant's Account of His Trial[97]

On the 18th day [after arriving in Block D], the prosecutor came to see and met with each of us [detainees] separately from 9:00 a.m. to 2:00 p.m. I asked why I was detained, what are the charges in Guantánamo . . . . The prosecutor wore civilian clothes. I only saw him once. He asked who caught me, why I was arrested . . . . I was told there would be no trial and the Guantánamo release paper will be recognized.[98]

Then he disappeared for three months . . . . By the end of my fourth month after I was visiting my family and returning to the cell I was told to go to the court instead. Ten people were brought to the court and told that they will be tried. I was accused of carrying an AK-47 and opposing the government. I rejected the charges. . . .There were three Afghan soldiers in the courtroom . . . . There were three judges . . . . The trial was 10-20 minutes. No evidence was shown . . . . I did not have a lawyer.

That day in the afternoon I was told the result and sentenced to five years . . . . But I have already spent four and a half years in Guantánamo and now four months in Block D.

I was given the sentence on a piece of paper and was told that I was sentenced to five years and that if I am unhappy with the decision then I could appeal.

* * * *

This Block D defendant was released one month after his conviction. His five-year sentence, it turned out, was to apply to "time served"—the length of time he already had spent in Guantánamo added to that in Block D. Although he was sentenced to time-served, the conviction by itself is punishment. He had no lawyer during the trial and was unable to challenge the evidence.

A copy of a Guantánamo Release Agreement from 2003 that accompanies a detainee upon release from U.S. custody is attached at Appendix E.

VI. Conclusion and Recommendations

Facilitating the transfer of U.S. detainees from indefinite imprisonment in Guantánamo and other U.S. detention facilities to the custody of their home country governments—provided there is no risk of torture or ill-treatment upon return—is one key way towards the ultimate closure of Guantánamo and other U.S. detention facilities. But the transfers have to be done responsibly. The Afghan experience provides insights into important steps that can be taken to improve the process for those transferred home for criminal prosecutions. Both the Afghan and U.S. governments have to ensure that trials are conducted according to international fair trial standards.

Human Rights First makes the following recommendations to the governments of Afghanistan and the United States:

To the United States Department of Defense

- Provide non-classified information, including exculpatory evidence, to the Afghan authorities to assist in criminal prosecutions. Specifically:

  - Make available to Afghan officials the names of soldiers or other personnel involved in the apprehension of each detainee, witnesses to the alleged offense, and personnel involved in any interrogation of the detainee resulting in admissions or statements relevant to alleged offenses by the detainees, and make soldiers and/or witnesses reasonably available for testimony, through video teleconference if necessary, for criminal proceedings; and

  - Provide Afghan authorities all statements by the transferred detainee; all reports, summaries, notes or other records of interrogation of the detainee; and any physical or documentary evidence in the possession of the U.S. government regarding each transferred detainee, including for example, notes, seized weapons or ammunition.

- Refrain from transferring any evidence obtained through coercion or cruel, inhuman or degrading treatment for use in criminal prosecutions by other governments.

- For detainees apprehended in the future: ensure that units participating in operations likely to result in the detention of civilians include personnel trained and equipped for elementary evidence collection procedures, in order to better ensure that detainees transferred to the Afghan government for prosecution can be lawfully prosecuted.

- Establish a legal support operation in Kabul to support the legitimate prosecution in Afghan courts of detainees transferred by the United States.

To the Afghan Attorney General's Office and the National Directorate of Security

- Request all relevant evidence in the possession of U.S. authorities, including exculpatory, regarding a detainee be turned over to Afghan officials at the time of transfer.

To the Afghan Supreme Court and Ministry of Justice

- Direct judges presiding over prosecutions of detainees transferred by the U.S. military to apply, and comply with, the Afghan criminal procedure code and international fair trial standards. Specifically, the Afghan courts in these cases should:

  - Ensure that defense counsel has access to all information that will be relied upon by the prosecution during trial;

  - Allow defense counsel to be present during the questioning of a defendant by the investigator and prosecutor prior to trial;

  - Require in-court witness testimony and allow cross-examination of witnesses by defense counsel; and

  - Refrain from relying upon any defendant's statement to U.S. or Afghan officials unless the defendant confesses in court under oath and without compulsion—as required by both the Afghan Constitution and criminal procedure code.

To the Afghan Supreme Court and Ministry of Defense

- Ensure that trials of former Guantánamo and Bagram defendants are open to observers, including family members and the media.

VII. Appendices

A. Glossary

ANA	Afghan National Army
ANDF	Afghan National Detention Facility
ANP	Afghan National Police
ARB	Administrative Review Board
BAF	Bagram Air Field
BITF	Bagram Theater Internment Facility
CAT	Convention against Torture
CCCI	Central Criminal Court of Iraq
CSRT	Combatant Status Review Tribunal
DOD	Department of Defense
ECRB	Enemy Combatant Review Board
EC	Enemy Combatant
ICRC	International Committee of the Red Cross
ICCPR	International Covenant of Civil and Political Rights
ICPC	2004 Interim Criminal Procedure Code for Courts
MOD	Afghan Ministry of Defense
MOJ	Afghan Ministry of Justice
NDS	National Directorate of Security
ROI	Report of Investigation
UNAMA	United Nations Assistance Mission in Afghanistan

B. 2008 Presidential Decree

Decree of President Karzai on the assignment of a delegation to evaluate the complains of the prisoners transferred from Bagram and Guantanamo

Anis (governmental newspaper), March 2

Based on the proposal of the Independent Commission of Peace Strengthening and to evaluate the complains of the prisoners, who have been transferred from Bagram and Guantanamo to Pul-e-Charkhi prison, an authorized delegation under the leadership of Mohammad Isahaq Alko and with the participation of the authorized representatives of the Supreme Court, Ministry of National Defence, National Directorate of Security and with the membership of the following individuals:

Mir Hayatullah, Advisor to the Commission of Peace Strengthening
Abdul Wahid Khamar, Advisor to the Commission of Peace Strengthening
General Abdul Salam Esmat, Head of Central Prison Department
Yar Mohammad, Prosecutor of the Investigation Section of the NDS Prosecution Office

are assigned to thoroughly and carefully check the complains, problems, documents and files of the prisoners transferred from the prisons in Guantanamo and Bagram and submit their report to the Presidency.

The National Directorate of Security and the other concerned judicial organs are tasked to provide the needed facilities to the delegation to perform their work.

C. Report of Investigation

UNCLASSIFIED

DETAINEE ASSESSMENT BRANCH
REPORT OF INVESTIGATION

DATE ROI PREPARED: 11 April 2007

SUBJECT: US9AF-002758DP Raieece ((MATELKY)),
Mohammed RAHIM, s/o FNU ((MATELKY))

    ETHNICITY: Pashtun
    TRIBE: Unknown
    LANGUAGE: Pashto

CO-SUBJECTS:

    1. US9AF-002760DP, AHMAD MARIED BAHARAN KHEL

VICTIM(S): Islamic Republic of Afghanistan (IRoA); Coalition Forces (CF)

OFFENSE(S): Anti Coalition Militia (ACM) Activity

DATE OF CAPTURE: 01 May 2006

JURISDICTION: Border Check Point, Tani District, Khost Province

SYNOPSIS: MATELKY was detained by Khost Police Forces and turned over to Coalition Forces on 01 May 2006 under suspicion of being part of a suicide bomber Improvised Explosive Device team. MATELKY was detained attempting to cross the border at a Border Check Point under suspicion of fleeing Afghanistan after the explosive device he was building was believed to have accidentally detonated and injured his accomplice. Their stories are conflicting and the Khost Police Force believe that they are directly tied to suicide attacks that were to take place during the Independence Day Parade in Khost.

CONFESSIONS/ADMISSIONS/INCRIMINATING STATEMENTS: None

WITNESSES: None

POTENTIAL WITNESSES:

    1. US9AF-002760DP, AHMAD MARIED BAHARAN KHEL

PHYSICAL EVIDENCE: None

PHOTOGRAPHS: None

Page 1 of 2
UNCLASSIFIED

Photo of detainee removed by Human Rights First

UNCLASSIFIED

MENTAL ILLNESS ISSUES: None

HEALTH ISSUES: See attached medical summary

POLYGRAPH: On 26 September 2006, SUBJECT was administered a specific issue polygraph examination. The result of the examination completed on this date was determined to be <u>Deception Indicated (DI)</u>.

    1. Have you been involved in any suicide bombing activities? (No.)

    2. Was Maried injured while making a suicide bombing vest? (No.)

During the pretest interview, the term "involved in any suicide bombing activities" was defined to mean planning suicide bombings; attending planning meetings; being recruited by Taliban or Al Qaeda to engage in suicide bombings; volunteering to engage in suicide bombings; being paid or offered compensation to engage in suicide bombings; purchasing or acquiring IED components, or financing suicide bombings; being trained in IED techniques or training others in IED techniques; or fabricating any type of suicide bombs.

MISCELLANEOUS:

    Current BTIF Behavior: Unfavorable, nuisance, disobedient.

ROI EXHIBITS: None

P.O.C. for this Assessment is CPT Daniel A. Zambrana, Detainee Assessment Branch Judge Advocate, DSN 231-2610.

D. Enemy Combatant Review Board Recommendation

US9AF-002758DP Raieece ((MATELKY)) s/o FNU ((MATELKY))
ECRB Recommended: Low Threat LLEC
POC: Border Check Point, Tani, Khost

<u>Capture Date</u>: 01 MAY 2006

Executive Summary: US9AF-002758DP was detained by Khost Police Forces (KPF) and turned over to CF on 01 May 2006 under suspicion of being part of a suicide bomber IED team. US9AF-002758DP was detained attempting to cross the border at a Border Check Point under suspicion of fleeing Afghanistan after the explosive device he was building was believed to have accidentally detonated and injured his accomplice. Their stories are conflicting and KPF believes that they are directly tied to suicide attacks that were to take place during the Independence Day Parade in Khost.

Evidence: Deception Indicated polygraph results on involvement in suicide attempts/assisting in suicide attacks.
Admittance or Denial: Denies involvement in insurgent activity.
BTIF Behavior: Unfavorable, nuisance, disobedient.
Current Assessment: Low Threat to US/CF / Low Prosecution value
NOTES:

Photo of detainee removed by Human Rights First

E. 2003 Guantánamo Release Agreement

AGREEMENT

WHEREAS, as a result of certain terrorist attacks, the United States and its coalition partners are engaged in armed conflict with al Qaida, an international terrorist organization, and its Taliban supporters; and

WHEREAS, _____ was detained as an enemy combatant during such armed conflict;

_____ undertakes as conditions for no longer being detained the following:

- THAT he will not in any way affiliate himself with al Qaida or its Taliban supporters;

- THAT he will not engage in, assist, or conspire to commit any combatant activities, or act in preparation thereof against the United States or its citizens, or against allies of the United States or citizens of such allies;

- THAT he will not engage in, assist, or conspire to commit any acts of terrorism or knowingly harbor anyone who does;

FURTHERMORE, _____ agrees that if he does not fulfill any of the above stated conditions, he may be detained immediately consistent with the law of armed conflict;

IN CONSIDERATION of these conditions, it is agreed that _____ will not be further detained by the United States, but should he not fulfill any of these conditions he may again be detained consistent with the law of armed conflict.

The agreement has been read to me and I understand the contents.

Signed this ___ day of _____, 200__

_____
Signature of Detainee to be released

_____
Appropriate U.S. Official

_____
Witness

_____
ISN# and Printed Detainee Name

11/20/2003

Release Agreement.doc

F. 1987 Internal and External Security Act

Democratic Republic of Afghanistan
Ministry of Justice
Official Gazette
Volume 14
Mizan 30

Decree of the Presidium of the Revolutionary Council of the Democratic Republic of Afghanistan
Kabul, No. 153

Regarding ratification of Law of Crimes Against the Internal and External Security of DRA.

The Presidium of the Revolutionary Council of Democratic Republic of Afghanistan approves the criminal provisions relating to crimes against internal and external security for consolidation of legality and better organization based on article (44) of the fundamental principals of DRA.

Article 1

The Law of Crimes Against Internal and External Security of DRA is ratified in two chapters and 30 articles.

Article 2

With the exception of article 25 and 26, investigation of crimes included in this law shall be implemented through the investigating organs of the Ministry of State Security.

Investigation of crimes in article 1 of this law with regard to ratification of the law of military crimes shall be carried out by the relevant organs within the limits of Article 2 of decree No.177 dated 9/11/1362 of the Presidium of the Revolutionary Council of Afghanistan.

Article 3

The Ministry of Justice of DRA together with the Ministry of State Security and other organs for protection of law shall prepare within one month a draft amendment to the law for discovery and investigation of crimes, and overseeing of its implementation by the attorney general office, in accordance with this law and send it for ratification to the Presidium of the Revolutionary Council.

Article 4

The Ministry of Justice of DRA prepares within fifteen days list of the criminal law provisions, which are to be annulled with the effective date of this law, and present it to the Presidium of the Revolutionary Council of DRA.

Article 5

This decree together with the law of crimes against the internal and external security of the DRA is ratified and comes into effect upon publication in the official gazette.

Haji Mohammad Chamkani in charge of the president of the presidium of the revolutionary council of DRA

Chapter One
Crimes Against Internal and External Security of the Democratic Republic of Afghanistan

Article 1
National treason against the country

1.   Treason is willful acts committed by a citizen of DRA against public sovereignty, safeguarding, territorial integrity, independence, national security and defense capability of the country as follow:

– Joining the enemy, armed activity against public sovereignty, spying, surrendering forces, turning over weapons, war techniques, fortifications and other facilities used for carrying out war, giving state and military secret information to countries or anti state organizations and or groups.

– Participating in and collaborating with foreign countries or anti state organizations or groups in carrying out hostile acts against DRA.

– Conspiring with the aim of taking over the state power.

– Perpetrator of crime of treason shall be sentenced to life imprisonment or death and confiscation of the property.

2.   If a citizen of DRA who has the intention of committing crimes included in this article or forced to commit these crimes, voluntarily informs the state authorities prior to committing the crime and prosecution, shall be exempt from punishment.

Article 2
Espionage

Stealing or collecting and hand over of secret information to foreign state, anti government organization or group or their agents, and collecting and submitting of other information by the order of foreign intelligence organs, which can be used against the

DRA, provided that the acts are performed by a foreign citizen and persons without citizenship, carry a sentence of life imprisonment or death and confiscation of the property.

Article 3
Terror

1. A person who kills a government political, social and religious personality representing the government, and ethnic and tribal chiefs in connection with their state or social duties, for purpose of weakening or destroying the public sovereignty, the perpetrator shall be sentenced to life imprisonment or death and confiscation of property.

2. If the person in clause one of this article is put under physical or psychological pressure for the purpose mentioned therein, the perpetrator shall be sentenced to imprisonment from three to ten years.

Article 4

1. If a person kills representative of a foreign country with the aim of instigating war or convulsion in diplomatic relations of DRA with other countries, the perpetrator shall be sentenced to life imprisonment or death penalty and confiscation of the property.

2. If the representative of a foreign country is put under physical or psychological pressure for the purpose mentioned herein, the perpetrator shall be sentenced to imprisonment from three to ten years.

Article 5
Destruction

1. If a person, with the aim of weakening public power and national economy, destroys institutions, communication lines, means of transport and communications and destroys or damages other government, social, cooperative and common or private properties by explosion or fire, or causes spread of epidemic diseases or mass poisonings, he shall be sentenced to imprisonment from ten to twenty years.

2. If committing of the acts mentioned in clause one of this article results in casualties or permanent disability, or cause substantial economic loss or grave consequences, the perpetrator shall be sentenced to life imprisonment or death penalty.

Article 6
Sabotage

1. If a person who intentionally or unintentionally uses public offices and social or private institutions with the aim of weakening or destroying the state authority, industry, trade, transport, agriculture, animal husbandry, financial order, communication means, or deranges other branches of national economy or activities of government organs, social, cooperative and mixed or private institutions, or prevents their regular activities, shall accordingly be sentenced imprisonment from three to ten years.

2. If committing of the acts result in major loss of national economy, the perpetrator shall be sentenced to long-term imprisonment.

Article 7
Propaganda against the government

1. A person who willfully disseminates false news, speeches, statements and self-interest calumny, or engages in provocative oral and written propaganda by any means, or have such publications in his possession, shall be sentenced to medium-term imprisonment.

2. If the acts mentioned in this article result in disruption of public order in government organs, institutions, public offices or disturb their regular work or ends in destruction, looting or fire, or committing these crimes is the result of contacts and communications or other means with anti government groups or hostile foreign government, the perpetrator shall be sentenced to long- term imprisonment.

3. If committing of the acts under this article lead to public chaos or loss of lives, the perpetrator shall be sentenced to life imprisonment or death.

Article 8
War propaganda

A person who spreads out war propaganda in any form, shall accordingly be sentenced to medium-term imprisonment.

Article 9
Organizational activity against internal and external security

1. A person who organizes, establishes, or administers undercover organization, group or body with the aim of committing crimes contained in chapter one of this law, shall be sentenced to life term imprisonment.

2. A person who becomes member of an organization mentioned in clause one of this article or its branch or subordinate, shall be sentenced to long-term imprisonment.

3. A person who himself or through another person establishes contacts with the branch or subordinate of organizations mentioned in clause one of this article for illegal purposes, or encourages others by intimidation or physical and psychological pressure, shall accordingly be sentenced to long- term imprisonment.

Article 10
Crimes against diplomatic relations of Afghanistan with foreign countries

If a person's action harms mutual relations of Afghanistan with foreign countries one way or another, he shall be sentenced to imprisonment from three to ten years.

If a person's action causes breakdown of diplomatic relations between Afghanistan and other countries, he shall be sentenced to life term imprisonment.

Chapter Two
Other crimes against internal and external security

Article 11
Violation of national, religious and racial equality rights

1. A person who engages in propagation to incite hostilities and national differences on racial, religious, ethnic and linguistic grounds, or makes efforts to limit the rights or ensures superiority of citizens based on ethnic, national, racial, religious, and linguistic differences, shall be sentenced to a medium-term imprisonment up to three years.

2. If such actions cause uprising or disorder among people, the perpetrator shall be sentenced to a long-term imprisonment.

Article 12
Command and control of armed forces units

A person who illegally takes over the command of unites of the armed forces and combat air craft with criminal intention,

without order of the responsible authorities and legitimate cause, or continues his action disregarding the order of the state to disengage, or keeps the soldiers assembled despite receiving order for laying down the weapons, shall be sentenced to life imprisonment or death penalty.

Article 13
Disclosing state secrets

A person who divulges the entrusted job related state secrets, or becomes aware of the secrets in the course of performing his duties without intention of treachery against the country, shall be sentenced to medium-term imprisonment.

If the action mentioned in part (1) of this clause has grave economic, political and military consequences for the Democratic Republic of Afghanistan, the person shall be sentenced to long-term imprisonment.

Article 14
Lost of documents containing governmental secrets

1. A person who loses secret government documents or materials handed over to him in connection with performing his duty, disregarding the regulations for keeping and preserving such documents, shall accordingly be sentenced to a medium-term imprisonment.

2. If the crime mentioned in part (1) of this clause causes grave consequences, the perpetrator shall be sentenced to long-term imprisonment.

Article 15
Armed robbery (Banditry)

The perpetrator of organizing armed robbery directed at the state offices, social institutions, economic institutions of joint stock, joint venture, cooperative nature and private personal offices constituted as banditry, shall be sentenced to long-term imprisonment.

Article 16
Taking hostage

1. If a person by use of threat, force or other means takes another person hostage shall be sentenced to long-term imprisonment and becomes liable for return of the same property, value or profit received thereof.

2. If the hostage is wounded, disabled or killed, the perpetrator shall be sentenced to long-term imprisonment and becomes liable for return of the same property, value or profit received thereof.

Article 17
Violation of international Flights

If entry or exit from airspace of the Democratic Republic of Afghanistan takes place without official permit, and non-observance of the authorized routes, landing airways, flight altitude or other violation of international flights, the perpetrator shall be sentenced to medium-term imprisonment.

Article 18
Illegal occupation of public institutions

A person who by using force occupies state buildings, institutions and other places built for public use, shall he sentenced to long-term or lifetime imprisonment.

Article 19
Counterfeiting and circulation of money and bonds

1. A person who counterfeits in any form the local currency and shareholder stocks in Afghanistan or foreign currencies, shall be sentenced to life-term imprisonment.

2. A person who knowingly circulates forged money and shareholder stocks or transacts, or has them in possession with the intention of circulation and dealings shall be sentenced to long-term imprisonment not exceeding ten years.

3. A person who knowingly brings into or sends out of Afghanistan forged money and shareholder stocks either himself or through another person, shall be sentenced to long-term imprisonment.

4. A person who makes, uses, sells, supplies or leases equipment and facilities used for forging money and shareholder stocks or have them in his possession, shall be sentenced to long-term imprisonment not less than ten years.

Article 20
Fundraising and assistance to anti state organization

A person who himself or through another person receives one way or another sums of money or any kind of benefit or material assistance from internal or external resources for committing crimes provided for in this law, shall accordingly be sentenced to long-term imprisonment.

Article 21
Illegal trade during war

1. If a person during war establishes trade relations personally or through his representative with a foreign government in war with the Democratic Republic of Afghanistan, or with the representative of the said government resided anywhere without consent of the Democratic Republic of Afghanistan, the goods thereof shall be subject to confiscation and he shall be sentenced to long term imprisonment not exceeding ten years.

2. If the subject goods under clause I of article 21 have not been confiscated, the court shall order the payment of its cost.

Article 22
Deferring commitment during war

1. If a person during war fails to perform all or part of his commitment for import and delivery of commodities to the government required by the armed forces or deliberately derange the essential food commodities for people, shall be sentenced to long-term imprisonment.

2. If the above-mentioned crimes lead to weakening the country's defense or operations of the armed forces, the perpetrator shall be sentenced to life imprisonment.

3. If a person during war defers carrying out of his assigned duties, shall be sentenced to medium-term imprisonment.

Article 23
Assisting the enemy forces

If a person for spiritual and material gains for himself or to another person serves the enemy forces directly or indirectly other than the conditions provided for in this law, shall be sentenced to long-term imprisonment not exceeding ten years.

Article 24
Insult the government flag and symbol

A person who publicly insults the flag or the symbol of the government of Afghanistan shall accordingly be sentenced to medium-term imprisonment.

Article 25
Provision and selling of goods for immorality

1. A person who for commercial purpose distributes, leases or supply press, literary work, drawings, slides, clichés, sculptures, portraits and coded signs repugnant to the culture and public manners or procure, import and export or have them in his possession shall accordingly be sentenced to imprisonment from one to three years.

2. In case, the acts stated in clause 1 of this article takes place for the purpose of moral corruption shall accordingly bear an imprisonment sentence from one to five years.

Article 26
Misuse and steal of cultural and ancient relics

1. Misuse and stealing of ancient cultural and written literary works, and use of publication, portraits, sculptures and other cultural and ancient relics belonging to the public, and also transfer, endowment and lease of them shall require an imprisonment sentence of one to three years.

2. Stealing, selling and causing to sell or intentional destruction of cultural relics shall require long-term imprisonment or compensatory cash penalty of equivalent in value.

Article 27
Non-reporting of crimes against internal and external security

If a person has reliable information on committing a crime such as act of treason, terror, espionage, obstructionism, war propaganda, organized anti government crimes and banditry and fails to report it to the public authorities shall be sentenced to medium-term imprisonment.

Article 28
Concealment of anti government and other crimes against national interests

If a person is aware of an anticipated crime such as treason, espionage, terrorism, destruction, obstructionism, organizing anti government crimes, banditry, counterfeiting of money and bonds and conceals it from others, shall be sentenced to medium-term imprisonment.

Article 29
Exemption from penal responsibility in accordance with this law

1. If a person after committing a crime and prior to legal prosecution provides to the relevant authorities information and full identification of the perpetrators or accomplices or other necessary information relevant to the disclosure of the crime, or introduces the accomplices of similar crimes to the authorities, the court shall observe extenuating circumstances in the case.

2. If a person reports to the relevant authorities before a crime is committed or prior to its completion, the informant shall be exempted from punishment.

Decree of the Executive Body of the Revolutionary Council of the Democratic Republic of Afghanistan

Kabul City No: 158 Dated: 26/05/1366

Regarding the approval of flag and symbol of Air Forces of the Democratic Republic of Afghanistan

In order to develop further and train the Air Forces personnel of the Democratic Republic of Afghanistan for occupational duties and morality amongst the air force personnel of the Democratic Republic of Afghanistan, the executive body of the revolutionary council of the Democratic Republic of Afghanistan approves the following:

1. To ratify the flag and symbol of the air forces of the Democratic Republic of Afghanistan.

2. To ratify the procedure for use of the flag of the Democratic Republic of Afghanistan.

G. Excerpts of 2004 Interim Criminal Procedure Code for Courts

Article 4
Presumption of Innocence

From the moment of the introduction of the penal action until when the criminal responsibility has been assessed by a final decision the person is presumed innocent. Therefore decisions involving deprivations or limitations of human rights must be strictly confined to the need of collecting evidence and establishing the truth.

Article 5
Suspect and Accused

1. A person is considered a suspect when in any deed of the investigations the commission of a crime is attributed to him.

2. A person is considered an accused when an act of indictment has been enacted by the Saranwal according to paragraph 4 of article 39.

3. The quality of accused remains until when the person is discharged or sentenced by a final decision.

4. The suspect and the accused shall not undergo intimidations or any form of physical or psychological pressure.

5. Their statements shall be made in a condition of absolute moral freedom.

6. The suspect and the accused have the right to abstain from making any statement even when they are questioned by the relevant police or judicial authorities.

7. The police, the Saranwal and the Court are duty bound to clearly inform the suspect and the accused before interrogation and at the time of arrest about his or her right to remain silent, right to representation at all times by defense counsel, and right to be present during searches, line-ups, expert examinations and trial.

8. The words or terms "suspect" and "accused" also include in their definition his/her defense counsel.

* * *

Article 19
Legal Aid

1. The suspect or the accused be financially unable to appoint a defense attorney are entitled to have a free defense attorney appointed for him or her in the following manner:

a. The investigating Saranwal or the Court adjudicating the case, on the petition of the person, appoints a defense attorney for the destitute person from amongst the lawyers officially permitted to work as defense attorney.

b. The person for whom an attorney has been appointed reserves the right not to accept the appointed defense attorney and to defend himself in person.

c. The fees of the aforesaid attorney shall be paid from the State budget and its extent shall be fixed by regulation.

Article 20
Interpreter

2. The suspect or the accused who does not know the language used during the investigations and the trials or who is deaf, dumb or deaf and dumb shall be given an interpreter for, at least, explaining to him the charge and the indictment and for assisting him during the interrogations and confrontations.

* * * *

Article 21
Reporting of Crimes

1. Police are duty bound to report within 24 hours to the Primary Saranwal all the crimes they happen to know.

2. Public officers are duty bound to report crimes ascertained in the performance of their duties.

3. Private citizens are duty bound to report to the judicial police or the Primary Saranwal only crimes against internal and external security.

Article 22
Institution of Proceedings

1. The Primary Saranwal has the obligation to introduce the penal action for prosecution of all crimes, known directly by him or reported to him, committed in the territory of the District, unless otherwise expressly provided by law.

2. The Saranwal shall not dismiss or stay a case except as otherwise provided by the law.

Article 23
Investigations

1. The Primary Saranwal performs the investigation activities by his own or making recourse to the collaboration of the judicial police.

2. The purpose of the criminal investigation is the establishment of the truth and in order to do so the Primary Saranwal shall extend his assessment to cover all facts and evidence relevant for establishing whether the crime has been committed and ascertaining who is responsible for it.

3. In conducting the investigations the Primary Saranwal is duty bound to evaluate incriminating and exonerating circumstances equally and to respect the interest of the victims.

* * * *

Article 33
Ratification of the Police's Decisions

1. The Primary Saranwal immediately after having been informed about the judicial police's activities indicated in articles 30, 31 and 32 either sanctions the deeds of the judicial police's activities or adopts decisions to revoke or modify them.

2. Before taking the actions mentioned in the previous paragraph the Saranwal can ask the police to provide explanations.

Article 34
Interrogation of the Person Arrested

1. The Primary Saranwal shall interrogate the person arrested within forty-eight hours from the moment when the person has been put at his disposal.

2. The Primary Saranwal can release the arrested suspect whenever he deems no more necessary the deprivation of liberty.

Article 35
Arrest and Seizures by the Primary Saranwal

1. In the course of the investigations activities the Primary Saranwal can order the arrest of the alleged author of a misdemeanor punishable by medium term imprisonment or felony and seizure of items and goods connected with the crime.

2. The person arrested shall be interrogated within forty-eight hours.

Article 36
Terms for Indictment in Case of Arrest

1. When the arrest performed by the Judicial Police is sanctioned or when the arrest has been ordered by the Saranwal and it remains in force, the arrested person shall be released if the Saranwal has not presented the indictment to the Court within fifteen days from the moment of the arrest except when the Court, at the timely request of the Saranwal, has authorized the extension of the term for not more than fifteen additional days.

Article 37
Collection of Evidence

1. During the investigations phase the Primary Saranwal shall collect all relevant evidence which can substantiate a decision pros or cons the suspect.

2. The collection of evidence is not restricted to particular forms or matters. The Primary Saranwal is free in selecting tools and modalities of proof.

3. The following shall be considered as key tools:

   a. Witnesses

   b. Confrontations

   c. Line up procedures

   d. Inspections

   e. Searches

   f. Seizure

   g. Expert exams and evaluations

   h. Interrogations

Article 38
Defense Counsel Presence

1. The defense counsel has the right to be present at all times during the interrogation of the suspect.

2. The suspect and the defense counsel have the right to be present during searches, confrontations, line-up procedures and expert examinations as well as during the trial.

3. In the investigation phase the Saranwal and the judicial police shall notify the suspect and his defense counsel of searches, confrontations, line-up procedures and expert examinations in order to allow them to be present. This duty can be waived only when there is an urgent need to conduct the said operations, which is defined as when it is a flagrante delicto crime or there is a fear of the loss of evidential facts.

Article 39
Conclusion of the Investigation

1. At the conclusion of the investigations phase, if the Primary Saranwal deems that there is not grounded evidence dismisses the case.

1. The victim or higher Saranwal can file a complaint to the Court against this decision within ten days.

2. The Court, after having examined the case, can confirm the decision of the Saranwal or vice versa request him to lodge the indictment.

3. In any other case the Saranwal shall submit to the Court the act of indictment requesting the assessment by trial of the criminal responsibility of the indicted person.

4. The act of indictment is comprised of the following:

   a. Complete identification of the suspect;

   b. Complete description of the crime.

5. Together with the act of indictment the Primary Saranwal shall transmit to the Court the file containing all the deeds formed during the investigations, putting at the Court's disposal the seized items and goods.

Article 40
Notification on the suspect

1. During the investigations the judicial police and the Saranwal shall give notifications of the deeds to the suspect, to his defense counsel and the victim of the activities to be accomplished, to which they have the right to be present.

2. If there are no particular grounded reasons of urgency, the notification should be served at least three days before the performance of the activity.

3. Reasons of urgency imposing a shorter period or absence of notifications shall be clearly mentioned in the record of the activities.

* * * *

Article 42
Preparation of the Trial

1. The Court immediately after having received the act of indictment, orders the notification of the deed indicating the day and hour fixed for the commencement of the trial.

2. The deed shall contain the name of the accused and the indication of the alleged crime with its factual circumstances in reference to the related law provisions and shall

be served on the accused and his defense counsel, the victim and the Saranwal at least five days in advance.

Article 43
Access of the Accused to the Findings of the Investigation

1. The accused and his defense counsel are entitled to examine the documents contained in the file mentioned in the last paragraph of article 39 and the objects under seizure.

* * * *

Article 49
Attendance of Witnesses and Experts

1. Witnesses and experts are duty bound to be present in the hearing indicated in the notification served on them.

2. If they do not appear without grounded justifications the Court orders their accompaniment by the police imposing on them a fine up to 500 Afghani.

* * * *

Article 51
Admission of Witnesses and Experts

1. The Primary Saranwal submits to the Court the list of the witnesses and experts he wants to be heard together with the act of indictment, indicating the reasons of the relevance of their testimony and exams.

2. The accused and/or his defense counsel have the right to present their own lists of witnesses and experts indicating the reasons of the relevance of their testimony and exams.

3. The Court can exclude those witnesses or experts that in its view do not appear material for the adjudication of the case.

4. The Court, on its own initiative, can order the appearance of witnesses or experts who are not included in the above mentioned lists.

Article 52
Order of the Hearing

1. The order of the hearing is explained to the persons present by the Head of the Court.

2. The court keeps the order of the hearing. Hearings are open to the public except when the court decides that all or part of it shall be run without the presence of the public for reasons of morality, family confidentiality or public order.

3. The Primary Saranwal, the accused and his defense counsel have the right to be always present.

4. The accused that with his behavior disrupts the proceedings can be excluded by the Court for part or all the duration of the hearing. He is anyhow readmitted in the room when the verdict is read out.

Article 53
Conduct of the Hearing

1. The Primary Saranwal is duty bound to take part in the hearing.

2. The accused and his defense counsel have the right to be present.

3. The Court proceedings are conducted according to the following order:

4. At the opening of the hearing the Court reads out the act of indictment;

5. When the accused is under detention the Court shall immediately assess the legality of the arrest and order the liberation of the accused when realizes that the arrest was unlawful or not necessary;

6. The Primary Saranwal makes an oral presentation of the case and of the findings of the investigations;

7. The judicial police officers who have conducted the investigations make oral reports of the activities accomplished;

8. The first witness to be heard is the victim;

9. Then the other witnesses and the experts are heard;

10. The accused can testify if he does not avail himself of the right to remain silent and the accused or his defense counsel can ask questions to the witnesses and the experts;

11. In case the witness cannot be present for health reasons the Court can hear him in his domicile;

12. The primary Saranwal and the defense lawyer can ask question to the accused.

13. The Court can, at any time, address questions to the accused, to any witness in the hearing and order confrontations.

14. The accused can refuse to answer the questions of the Court consistent with his right to remain silent.

* * * *

Article 55
Evidentiary Value of Investigative Activities

1. The records of the testimonies of the witnesses as well as of the expert exams, collected during the investigative phase, can have the value of evidence as basis for the decision only if it results that the accused and/or his defense counsel were present during the operations and were in a position to raise questions and make objections.

2. Otherwise the related deeds have the sole value of clues.

* * * *

Article 58
Conclusion of the Trial

1. At the conclusion of the operations indicated in the previous articles, the Primary Saranwal expresses his opinion requesting the Court to make a decision of dismissal or sentence, indicating the kind and the amount of punishment he deems adequate.

2. The accused or the defense counsel, when present, submits to the Court arguments in rebuttal of the accusation.

Article 59
Decision of the Court

1. At the completion of the activities, the Court declares the closing of the hearing and leaves the trial room for writing down 'in chamber' the decision of the case.

2. Later on, the Court enters the trial room again and reads out the verdict together with its reasons. This reading has the value of notification. If the reasons of the verdict are not read out by the Court in the same context, they shall be deposited in the office of the secretary of the Court within fifteen days from the moment of the decision.

3. The Primary Saranwal, the accused and his defense counsel shall receive notification of the deposit indicated in paragraph 2 of this article.

4. The accused tried in absentia, in the case of article 47, shall receive notification of the decision read out by the Court together with the reasons deposited later on in the office of the secretary of the Court.

5. The notification indicated in the previous paragraph is served on the defense counsel of the accused in the case of article 46.

VIII. Endnotes

[1] Secretary of Defense Robert Gates told a House of Representatives committee that he wanted the Guantánamo prison to be closed and the trials moved to the United States "because I felt that no matter how transparent, no matter how open the trials, if they took place in Guantánamo, in the international community they would lack credibility." BBC, "Gates Urges Closure of Guantánamo," BBC News, March 29, 2007, http://news.bbc.co.uk/2/hi/americas/6508779.stm. In March 2008, five former Secretaries of State, Collin Powell, Henry Kissinger, James Baker III, Warren Christopher and Madeleine Albright, all called for Guantánamo to be closed. Greg Bluestein, "5 Ex-Chief Diplomats: Close Guantanamo," Associated Press, March 28, 2008.

[2] Ambassador Thomas Schweich, Coordinator on Counternarcotics and Justice Reform in Afghanistan, at panel discussion on "Afghanistan: Bringing the Rule of Law to a War-Torn Country," New York, March 20, 2008.

[3] This number was calculated based on Department of Defense news releasees announcing detainee transfers to Afghanistan on March 1, 2007, April 26, 2007, August 9, 2007, September 29, 2007, November 4, 2007, and December 12, 2007.

[4] Out of the 15 detainees charged, David Hicks, pled guilty in a pre-trial agreement and was returned to Australia in April 2007 to serve his 9-month sentence. The other 14 detainees facing charges are currently still held at Guantánamo.

[5] Military Commissions Act of 2006, 10 U.S.C. §948(a)(1) (2006).

[6] U.S. Department of State, Second Periodic Report of the United States of America to the Committee Against Torture, U.N. Doc. CAT/C/48/Add.4, Annex, Part One, §II(A), June 2005.

[7] See Human Rights First, "Human Rights First Analyzes DoD's Combatant Status Review Tribunals," August 2004, http://www.humanrightsfirst.org/us_law/detainees/status_review_080204.htm; Human Rights First, "Six Years without Judicial Review: CSRTs Not an Adequate Substitute for Habeas Review," December 2007, http://www.humanrightsfirst.org/us_law/detainees/miltcom_jud_review.htm

[8] The ARB was instituted "as a matter of discretion" by the Secretary of Defense who "may suspend or amend" its procedures, at anytime, thereby indicating that they are not independent. The ARB scheme is not subject to judicial review, does not have the authority to change the "enemy combatant" classification, and cannot require the release of a detainee. U.S. Department of Defense, Order establishing Administrative Review Procedures for Enemy Combatants in the Control of the Department of Defense at Guantanamo Bay Naval Base, Cuba, May 11, 2004, section 6, p.9, http://www.defenselink.mil/news/May2004/d20040518gtmoreview.pdf

[9] Ruzatlullah v. Donald Rumsfeld, Declaration of Colonel Rose Miller, Commander, Task Force Guardian, Combined Joint Task Force 76, No. 06-CV-01707, (D. D.C. November 19, 2006), para. 11.

[10] Ibid.

[11] Ibid.

[12] Human Rights First telephone interview with Tina Foster, International Justice Network, New York, March 25, 2008. International Justice Network has filed habeas corpus petitions on behalf of Bagram detainees in U.S. courts.

[13] U.S. President George W. Bush and Afghan President Hamid Karzai, "Joint Declaration of the United States-Afghanistan Strategic Partnership," White House news release, May 23, 2005, http://www.whitehouse.gov/news/releases/2005/05/20050523-2.html.

[14] Ibid.

[15] Ibid.; *see also*, Kenneth Katzman, *Afghanistan: Post-War Governance, Security, and U.S. Policy*, Congressional Research Service Report for Congress, RL30588, January 28, 2008.

[16] U.S. Embassy, Kabul, Afghanistan, "Detainee Transfers to Afghanistan," press release, August 4, 2005, http://kabul.usembassy.gov/pr080405.html (accessed February 15, 2008).

[17] Tim Golden, "Foiling US Plans, Prison Expands in Afghanistan, *New York Times*, January 18, 2008; NBC News, U.S. eyes Afghan jail for some Gitmo detainees, June 22, 2007, http://www.msnbc.msn.com/id/19358932/ (accessed March 12, 2008).

[18] Golden, "Foiling US Plans, Prison Expands in Afghanistan."

[19] U.N. Special Representative of the Secretary-General for Afghanistan, *Agreement on Provisional Arrangements in Afghanistan Pending the Re-establishment of Permanent Government Institutions*, U.N. Doc. S/2001/1154, II.2 (Bonn, Germany: December 5, 2001) (hereafter Bonn Agreement). The Bonn Agreement mandated the establishment of an Afghan Judicial Commission to review the functions of the justice system, facilitate law reform, strengthen technical, logistical, and human resources, expand legal aid, and promote access to justice.

[20] Bonn Agreement, II.2.

[21] United Nations Development Programme, Afghanistan Human Development Report 2007, *Bridging Modernity and Tradition: Rule of Law* (Pakistan: Center for Policy and Human Development, 2007).

[22] Combined Security Transition Command-Afghanistan, CSTC-A Fact Sheet, December 1, 2007, http://www.cstc-a.com/mission/CSTC-AFactSheet.html (accessed February 25, 2008). The CSTC-A's mission statement states that it "in partnership with the Government of the Islamic Republic of Afghanistan and the international community, is to plan, program and implement . . . reforms of the Afghan National Security Forces in order to develop a stable Afghanistan, strengthen the rule of law, and deter and defeat terrorism within its borders."

[23] U.S. Department of State, Bureau for International Narcotics and Law Enforcement Affairs, Civilian and Rule of Law Programs, Fact Sheet, January 2, 2008, http://www.america.gov/st/texttrans-english/2008/January/20080102125641eaifas0.5786402.html (accessed February 27, 2008).

[24] Ibid.; *see also* Testimony of Anne W. Patterson, Assistant Secretary for International Narcotics and Law Enforcement Affairs before the House Committee on Appropriations Subcommittee on Foreign Operations, Export Financing and Related Programs, September 12, 2006, http://www.state.gov/p/inl/rls/rm/72241.htm (accessed February 28, 2008) (U.S. criminal justice experts train and mentor judges, prosecutors, and defense counsel in criminal procedures, cases, and trials).

[25] Human Rights First interview with U.S. Embassy official (name withheld), Kabul, February 6, 2008.

[26] Ibid.

[27] Human Rights First interview with national security prosecutor (name withheld) Kabul, February 4, 2008.

[28] Ibid.

[29] Ibid. According to the Afghan government, the National Commission for Peace and Reconciliation has disarmed more than 6,000 Taliban members. *See* Embassy of Afghanistan, News and Views: Prof. Sibghatullah Al-Mojadeddi Travels to U.S. for National Prayer Breakfast, http://www.embassyofafghanistan.org/02.12.2008usip.html (accessed March 3, 2008).

[30] Golden, "Foiling U.S. Plans, Prison Expands in Afghanistan."

[31] The National Security Council (NSC) established by presidential decree advises the president on security-related issues and develops and coordinates Afghan security policy.

[32] Decree of President Hamid Karzai, March 2, 2008.

[33] Human Rights First telephone interview with committee member (name withheld), April 7, 2008.

[34] Ibid.

[35] Human Rights First interview with ANA official (name withheld), Pul-i-Charkhi, February 4, 2008.

[36] *See, e.g.*, United Nations, "The Situation in Afghanistan and its implications for international peace and security," Report of the U.N. Secretary-General, March 6, 2008, U.N. Doc. A/62/722-S/2008/159; United Nations, Report of the U.N. Secretary-General, "The Situation in Afghanistan and its implications for international peace and security," U.N. Doc. A/62/345-S/2007/555, September 21, 2007; *see also*, Amnesty International, *Afghanistan: Detainees Transferred to Torture: ISAF Complicity?* November 13, 2007.

[37] Human Rights First interview with ANA official (name withheld), Pul-i-Charkhi, February 4, 2008.

[38] Ibid.

[39] Ibid.

[40] Ibid.

[41] Human Rights First interviews with family members of Guantanamo detainees (names withheld), Kabul, February 1, 2008.

[42] ICRC News Release, Afghanistan: Video links between Bagram detainees and families, http://www.icrc.org/Web/Eng/siteeng0.nsf/html/afghanistan-news-140108!OpenDocument.

[43] Human Rights First interviews with family members of Guantanamo detainees (names withheld), Kabul, January 29, 2008, January 31, 2008, and February 1, 2008.

[44] Human Rights First interview with brother of Guantanamo detainee (name withheld), Kabul, January 29, 2008.

[45] Human Rights First interviews with family members of Guantanamo detainees (names withheld), Kabul, January 29, 2008, January 31, 2008, and February 1, 2008.

[46] Human Rights First interviews with family members of Guantanamo detainees (names withheld), Kabul, January 29, 2008, January 31, 2008, and February 1, 2008.

[47] Human Rights First interview with brother of Guantanamo detainee (name withheld), Kabul, January 29, 2008.

[48] Mark Sedra, Geneva Center for the Democratic Control of Armed Forces, *Security Sector Transformation in Afghanistan*, Working Paper No. 143, August 2004, http://www.dcaf.ch/_docs/WP143.pdf (accessed February 22, 2008).

[49] United Nations Office at Geneva, "High Commissioner for Human Rights Concludes Visit to Afghanistan," press release, November 20, 2007, http://www.unog.ch/80256EDD006B9C2E/(httpNewsByYear_en)/05C1CDC5973400F6C1257399005AC271?OpenDocument (accessed March 12, 2008).

[50] Human Rights First interviews with defense lawyers (names withheld), Kabul, February 3, 3008, and Human Rights First interview national security prosecutor (name withheld), Kabul, February 4, 2008.

[51] Interim Criminal Procedure Code for Courts, Official Gazette No. 820, February 25, 2004, art. 22-23, 37.

[52] Ibid., art. 23.

[53] Ibid., art. 39, 55.

[54] Human Rights First interview with defense lawyer (name withheld), Kabul, January 30, 2008.

[55] Human Rights First interview with defense lawyer (name withheld), Kabul, February 2, 2008.

[56] Human Rights First interview with defense lawyer (name withheld), Kabul, February 2, 2008.

[57] Human Rights First interview with national security prosecutor (name withheld), Kabul, February 4, 2008.

[58] Ibid.

[59] Human Rights First interview with former Block D defendant (name withheld), Kabul, January 30, 2008. Article 38(1) of the ICPC provides defense counsel the right to be present at all times during the interrogation of the suspect.

[60] Human Rights First interview with defense lawyer (name withheld), Kabul, January 30, 2008.

[61] Human Rights First interview with judge (name withheld), Kabul, February 5, 2008.

[62] Human Rights First interview with U.S. embassy official (name withheld), Kabul, February 6, 2008.

[63] Human Rights First interview with defense lawyer (name withheld), Kabul, February 2, 2008.

[64] Human Rights First interview with judge (name withheld), Kabul, February 4, 2008.

[65] Human Rights First interview with official from National Peace and Reconciliation Commission (name withheld), Kabul, January 28, 2008.

[66] Human Rights First interview with brother of Guantanamo detainee (name withheld), Kabul, January 29, 2008.

[67] Human Rights First interview with brother of Guantanamo detainee (name withheld), Kabul, January 29, 2008.

[68] International Covenant of Civil and Political Rights, December 16, 1966, 999 U.N.T.S. 171, art. 14(1).

[69] Ibid., art. 14(3)(a-g).

[70] European Court of Human Rights, *Kostovski v. The Netherlands* (App. 11454/85), Judgment of 20 November 1989; (1990) 12 EHRR 434; D.J. Harris, M. O'Boyle and C. Warbrick, Law of the European Convention on Human Rights (London: Butterworths) (1995), p. 212.

[71] ICPC, art. 38(2-3). Article 37 of the Afghan Interim Criminal Procedure Code allows the primary *saranwal* to "collect all relevant evidence," including witnesses, confrontations, line up procedures, inspections, searches, seizures, expert evaluations, and interrogations. Defense counsel and the defendant have the right to examine the documents in the dossier and any objects captured during seizure. ICPC, art. 43.

[72] ICPC, art. 55.

[73] Human Rights First interview with defense lawyer (name withheld), Kabul, February 2, 2008.

[74] Human Rights First interview with national security prosecutor (name withheld), Kabul, February 4, 2008.

[75] Ibid.

[76] *See* Major W. James Annexstad, "The Detention and Prosecution of Insurgents and Other Non-Traditional Combatants—A Look at the Task Force 134 Process and Future of Detainee Prosecutions," *Army Lawyer*, July 2007.

[77] See, e.g., Human Rights First, Tortured Justice: Using Coerced Evidence to Prosecute Terrorist Suspects, March 2008, at http://www.humanrightsfirst.info/pdf/08307-etn-tortured-justice-web.pdf; Human Rights First and Physicians for Human Rights, Leave No Marks: Enhanced Interrogation Techniques and the Risk of Criminality, August 2007, at http://www.humanrightsfirst.info/pdf/07801-etn-leave-no-marks.pdf;

Human Rights First, Command's Responsibility: Detainee Deaths in U.S. Custody in Iraq and Afghanistan, February 2006, at http://www.humanrightsfirst.info/pdf/06221-etn-hrf-dic-rep-web.pdf; U.N. Commission on Human Rights, Sixty-First session, Report of the independent expert on the situation of human rights in Afghanistan, M. Cherif Bassiouni," U.N. Doc. E/CN.4/2005/122, March 11, 2005.

[78] See, e.g., Dan Eggen and R. Jeffery Smith, "FBI Agents Allege Abuse of Detainees at Guantanamo Bay," *Washington Post*, December 21, 2004 (citing FBI documents obtained by the American Civil Liberties Union through Freedom of Information Act litigation); Dana Priest and Barton Gellman, "U.S. Decries Abuse But Defends Interrogations," *Washington Post*, December 26, 2002; Associated Press, "U.S. General: Details in probe of Afghan jails to stay secret," June 1, 2004.

[79] James R. Schlesigner, et al., *Final Report of the Independent Panel to Review DoD Detention Operations* (August 2004), http://www.defenselink.mil/news/Aug2004/d20040824finalreport.pdf; Department of Defense, *Review of DoD Detention Operations and Detainee Interrogation Techniques, Executive Summary* (March 2005), http://www.defenselink.mil/news/Mar2005/d20050310exe.pdf.

[80] Human Rights First interview with former Block D defendant (name withheld), Kabul, January 30, 2008.

[81] Verbatim Transcript of Combatant Status Review Tribunal Hearing for ISN 874 [Abdul Nasir], CSRT Set 47, Enclosure (3), March 3, 2006, p. 3134-3139; Verbatim Transcript of Administrative Review Board for ISN 874 [Abdul Nasir], ARB Set 9, Enclosure (6), p. 21084-21093.

[82] Golden, "Foiling US Plans, Prison Expands in Afghanistan."

[83] See generally, Human Rights First, *Tortured Justice*, February 2008.

[84] Human Rights First interview with defense lawyer (name withheld), Kabul, February 2, 2008.

[85] Human Rights First interview with defense lawyer (name withheld), Kabul, February 2, 2008.

[86] Constitution of Afghanistan, January 3, 2004, art. 30.

[87] ICPC, art. 5(4).

[88] The Convention against Torture and Other Cruel, Inhuman or Degrading Treatment or Punishment, for example, ratified by Afghanistan in 1987 and the U.S. in 1994, states that "[e]ach state party shall ensure that any statement which is established to have been made as a result of torture shall not be invoked as evidence in any proceedings." Convention against Torture, June 26, 1984, 1465 U.N.T.S. 85, art. 15.

[89] Human Rights First interview with Block D defendant (name withheld), Kabul, January 30, 2008.

[90] Human Rights First interview with U.S. Embassy official (name withheld), Kabul, February 6, 2008.

[91] Human Rights First interview with defense lawyer (name withheld), Kabul, February 2, 2008.

[92] Human Rights First interview with defense lawyer (name withheld), Kabul, February 2, 2008.

[93] Human Rights First interview with defense lawyer (name withheld), Kabul, February 2, 2008.

[94] ICPC, art. 20.

[95] ICCPR, art. 14(3).

[96] Human Rights First interview with official from Supreme Court (name withheld), Kabul, February 2, 2008.

[97] Human Rights First interview with Block D defendant (name withheld), Kabul, January 30, 2008.

[98] The Guantánamo Release Agreement does not state whether a detainee is innocent or guilty but sets forth conditions for release—namely that the detainee will not engage in hostilities against the U.S. or its allies, will not be affiliated with al Qaeda or the Taliban, and will not engage in terrorist attacks. The Release Agreement states that the U.S. will no longer detain that person but can do so at a later date if the conditions are violated.

www.ingramcontent.com/pod-product-compliance
Lightning Source LLC
Chambersburg PA
CBHW081724290326
41933CB00053B/3308